"A SEARCH FOR LOVE"

"A SEARCH FOR LOVE"

Janice Stampley Means

iUniverse, Inc.
Bloomington

"A SEARCH FOR LOVE"

iUniverse books may be ordered through booksellers or by contacting:

iUniverse
1663 Liberty Drive
Bloomington, IN 47403
www.iuniverse.com
1-800-Authors (1-800-288-4677)

ISBN: 978-1-4759-7968-8 (sc)
ISBN: 978-1-4759-7969-5 (ebk)

Printed in the United States of America

iUniverse rev. date: 02/28/2013

Dedication

TO MY LORD AND SAVIOR, JESUS CHRIST

"Thank you for allowing me to be one of yours"

TO MY LOVING FAMILY

&

THE LATE HARDY AND DOROTHY STAMPLEY

Preface

My name is Janice Stampley Means and I'm a resident of Boiling Springs S. C. I'm also the mother of two sons and the estranged wife of a currently incarcerated husband. I'm also focusing on and maintaining my independence from a gambling addiction. Over the years I've struggled to survive the trials and tribulations of my life. And I've come to the realization that I can only do it through Christ Jesus who strengthens me. Because of these struggles God has given me an opportunity to share my testimonies through Poetry and Prose. I'm proud to say that God has given me the courage and conviction to go out and share my testimonies with others. I've recently been blessed to write three Poetry books titled "Poetry for the Soul vol. 1, 2 and 3". These poems touch on a range of topics including Gods grace, addictions, abuse and neglect. God has anointed me to write these powerful poems and prose in effort to be a comfort to others in their time of need. Because everyone will encounter a time in their life where they will need some encouragement.

And these books will show that through Gods grace and mercy everyone has the power to survive. Through these books I was not only given a form of self healing but it also encouraged me to present my story in hope that I could give strength and encouragement to others in their time of need.

"A SEARCH FOR LOVE"

*M*y life began in a small town called Natchez, M.S., I was born in 1968 at the Charity Hospital and was the 3rd child of six siblings. I grew up deep in the country where a crowing rooster awakened each household every morning. As a child I attended Sunday school & church every Sunday, mostly because my mother was the Sunday school teacher. I had a very close relationship with my mother; she taught me everything I needed to know about taking care of myself. She always emphasized the importance in cooking and cleaning, because she didn't want us to ever have to depend on a man. I enjoyed my childhood to the fullest, especially in Jr. High School. I ran track so my mother would take us to the Natchez Trace, where we could play ball or race against each other.

My life took a change of events when my parents started having marital problems. My father was seeing another woman and eventually began abusing my mother. His betrayal caused him to curse at her constantly for no reason; and one day I witnessed my mother taking him some food only for him to throw it against the wall. But that was only the beginning because shortly after that they began fighting all the time. And my siblings and I would try to break it up, only to be knocked to the floor. I often wondered why my mother didn't leave him, because I knew she couldn't be happy living this way. And after it seemed like an eternity of watching her being abused she finally got the nerve to leave. But we didn't have anywhere to go so she asked my father's sister "Could we stay with them." Everything was fine for a while and eventually my mother met someone; but I knew she was still depressed because I would always hear her crying during the night.

Shortly before Christmas my mother left the house walking because she was depressed about not having any money to buy Christmas gifts. But that night she met a man and they went out for coffee and she told him about her situation. And a week later she received a letter in the mail with a thousand dollars informing her to buy us something for Christmas. That was the happiest I'd seen my mother in a long time. Eventually she started going out of town to see this mysterious man, but as long as she was happy we was happy. For a while everything seemed to be going good, we moved into our own house and my mother had finally put the past behind her. But for some reason she had become very protective over her girls, she said" It was vital that we learn how to cook & clean so that we can take care of ourselves." She also use to make our older brother watch us whenever there were boys around. We couldn't sit in the living room and talk to a boy without our brother walking back & forth all night. But it was for the best because it kept us from moving too fast and getting pregnant.

But my mother was having problems of her own with the previous guy she had met. We didn't think it was serious because he was a very quiet and harmless looking man. But she was trying to break up with him, so she could be with the mysterious man she had met the night she went walking.

But one night during the summer of 84 my mother's life was tragically taken; her friend blew her brains out after telling her "If I can't have you no one will." On that tragic night me & one of my sisters was in New Orleans visiting our aunt when we received the news. It felt like my heart had temporarily stopped beating; I couldn't even make myself cry. On the trip back home it seemed like everything was going in slow motion; it felt as though a part of my soul had left my body.

Reality didn't set in until I made it home, and just to see the room where she had been shot literally tore my heart to pieces. When I went to bed that night I couldn't make myself stop crying.

Every time I would close my eyes I would see my mom's face. It seemed like the funeral was the very next day; I still couldn't believe this was really happening. The last thing I remember was looking at my mother's body & feeling light headed. When I woke up I was back at the house, and noticed someone had laid me across my mother's bed. All I could do was hold her pillow and cry. I didn't know how to handle this situation so I blamed God for everything.

Things were moving very fast after my mother's funeral; I recalled seeing people taking photos and other keepsakes before they left. We didn't want to be separated so our grandmother said "We could remain at the house and she would become guardian over us." She said "she would come and check on us every day", but after a while her visits slowed down and eventually stopped. So we came to the conclusion that we had to take care of ourselves. Our older brother was currently working at Churches Chicken and brought us leftovers home each night. Eventually that wasn't enough and we had to resort to stealing food, clothing and feminine products. And since no one was watching us, we did everything a typical unsupervised teenager would do. One night my friend and I had some boys over to the house, and by them being much older they tried to offer us some drugs. My friend decided to try some, but when it was offered to me I flat out refused.

And after sniffing one of the lines, she immediately fell to the floor. That was all I had to see to know that drugs was not for me.

It seemed like after my mother's death there was no one to show me any love. And after a while my heart hardened, and I stopped showing love also. The pain had begun to hurt so bad that I eventually started drinking and hanging out. It seemed like every time I felt the pain of my mother's death I would drink more and more. I soon stopped caring about anything or anyone. I had become so rebellious that my grandmother didn't know what to do with me. I realized the alcohol had taken over when I found myself fighting all the time. It felt like I had no control over my own emotions, and every time I would fight I would end up in jail. But every time I went to jail it only intensified the hatred I felt for the world. And it made me blame God more and more for everything that had happened, but mostly for taking away the only person I ever loved. I felt so alone and lost and it didn't help matters any to find out that my father had told my siblings "Not to call him if I go to jail anymore." I held a deep resentment toward him for that, because even though I was a problem child I still felt he should have been there for me.

One night my friend and I went to the club, and after drinking too much she got in a fight. And since we were there together I jumped in to help her. Very soon a crowd had formed, and someone said "Break it up she's bleeding." But at the time I didn't know it was me, I thought I was just sweating but it was actually blood on my face. People began screaming and saying "Someone call an ambulance." By then I asked my friend to let me see my face, and when I looked in the mirror I couldn't believe that was me.

I had a hole in my face and a cut on my head, and a cut across my windpipe and several other places. When I arrived at the hospital everything was moving so fast, the nurse came in almost passed out and that really scared me. I felt as though I was being tortured, because they were giving me shots in my head & throat and at the same time so that I could receive stitches. By this time my siblings had arrived at the hospital, and I heard the doctor tell my family "Not to let me look in a mirror, because I would probably go into shock." I'll never forget that date; it was February 3rd on my brother's birthday, I received 96 stitches & plates in my upper body. And by me being a minor at the time the state offered to give me plastic surgery at no cost to me, but I was scared and refused to have it.

During the next 6 months it was real hard for me, because I couldn't sleep in my bed because of the stitches I had in my neck & my head. I wasn't able to eat anything but liquid soup, and it had to be sucked through a straw. By the time my stitches were taken out I was small as a broom stick, and even though I was embarrassed I started going back to school.

During the next few years I slowed down until I got completely healed. But at the same time my resentment and anger was growing stronger & stronger, and I still hadn't found the love I so desired. One day my sister and I was out taking care of some business, and I saw the lady that had cut me and I attempted to assault her, but the security guard grabbed me and I was taken to jail. At this point I was not only furious with the world but with my family also. No one came to see me for that whole week because of my conduct. So I calmed down so they would think I was alright but the anger and hurt was still there. One night I was sitting at home and began to cry, and asked God "Why did he let me live?" And why did he take the only person I ever loved?" At this point I felt I needed someone that I could love and that would love me back. That was the first time I had talked to God in years.

Then one day a friend of my mother's came to visit, and I asked her "Could I come stay with her for a little while," and she said "Yes." But while I was there, I decided it would be best if I stayed away from my old surroundings, so I got her to enroll me into Fayette High School. And one day I was sitting outside and noticed this guy walking up and down the sidewalk listening to his radio. I never would've thought I would end up dating him, but that's exactly what happened. After being introduced we started seeing a lot of each other, and eventually began dating. After dating for a while we decided to take our relationship a little further. I was still a virgin and the thought of sex was intriguing but also scary. But I still remembered my conversation with God about wanting someone to love me and that I could love in return. So I decided to sleep with him, but not before letting him know up front that I wanted to get pregnant. And since my mother had passed when I was young, I was never taught about sex and babies. So I asked this older lady "What can I take to help me get pregnant quicker?" And she said "To take some geritol pills because they'll make my body fertile enough to get pregnant."

So one night while his mother was gone I came over and we made love.

I was shaking like a leaf on a tree; I couldn't believe what I was feeling the pain was so unbearable. But all I could think of was how bad I wanted a baby so it was worth it. When my mom's friend found out what had happened she was furious, and threatened to send me back to Natchez. I cried all night because I didn't want to leave my boyfriend, so I asked his mom "Could I stay with them until I finished my school year." I knew she would agree because she was an open-minded type of mother. She knew her son and I had already slept together, so she didn't say too much. After staying there for a while she actually allowed us to sleep together all the time. Everything was great, I was able to go to school and play house at the same time. Eventually he wanted a baby just as much as I did; even though we had our own reasons. Mine was to have someone to love, and his was to use the baby to hold onto me. For a while it seemed like we were having sex every day. And eventually I began sleeping all the time and his mother said "I guess now ya'll have your wish." I made an appointment with the doctor and he confirmed my pregnancy. That was the happiest news I could've ever received, despite the fact I didn't know anything about being pregnant.

By now I was going to the 12th grade, and decided I wanted to do my last year at home. So me and my baby's father packed our things and went to live in Natchez. Everything was fine until my labor pains became so unbearable that I had drop out of school. But in July of 87 at 5:55am I brought a handsome little boy into this world. My baby's father and I was so happy because we both had gotten what we wanted. But after I got well I got caught stealing and ended up in jail again. Even though I had been to jail before this time was different, because now I was being taken away from my child. So at that moment I promised myself that I would never do anything to get taken away from my child again. I went back to school in 88 and completed my 12th grade year with one of my younger sisters. The day I graduated I was so proud of myself, because my siblings, my boyfriend and my son was all there to see me accept my diploma. Shortly after graduation I had gotten tired of living in Mississippi, and since my brother had gotten married and was moving to North Carolina I asked "Could we go." They said "Yes" but I would have to go alone because they couldn't accommodate a whole family." And even though it was hard I knew this was my only chance to go and start a new life for us in a new city. So I sent my baby and his father back to Fayette to stay with his mother until I could return for them. The day I got on the greyhound I felt so bad having to leave my baby and his dad behind. I sit directly behind the driver so he could help me with my transfers until I reached my destination. I was excited but also scared because I had never been that far from home before. I know we rode about 23 hours that day and I cried the whole trip. Once I arrived my brother picked me up at the bus station and informed me "That my baby's dad had called several times already." That made me happy because I knew he was missing me. I was homesick already and it was only the first day, because even though my baby couldn't talk yet I would have given anything to hear his voice.

The next day I went job hunting because I knew the sooner I start working the quicker I could get my family up here. I immediately got a job at a nursing home called Hill Haven and a job at Long John Silver. I decided to work 2 jobs so that I could get my family up here as soon as possible. I talked to my baby's father every night so he could keep me informed on what was going on with our child. One night after work I received a phone call and heard a voice say "ma' ma," tears immediately filled my eyes because those were the most precious words I could ever hear. And when he told me "Our son had taken his first steps," I wanted to go home so bad I could have died. The next day I went and applied for an apartment in housing, but while I was out I ran across a one bedroom efficiency apartment. It was very small but I took it because I was ready to get my family up here. And within two months I had made enough money to go and get them. When I arrived at the bus station in Fayette, I could see my boyfriend and my baby waving at me. That night we cried together because it seemed as though we had been apart a lifetime. We stayed a couple of days with his mother and then caught the bus back to North Carolina to start our new life together. I was excited when we arrived because I was ready to show them our new home. It wasn't much but it was beautiful to us because it was a place where we could be together.

The next day my brother hired my boyfriend at the KFC close to our house. It worked out fine because by my brother being the manager he would give us the leftovers each night. And that helped us out a lot because it provided us with food, and that was an expense we didn't have to worry about. My sister-in-laws aunt also helped out by taking us everywhere we needed to go. She and her husband treated us like family and we loved them for that. She took me to apply for stamps and to buy a few odds and ends for my apartment. Everything was going good but our apartment was beginning to get too small, so I called to check on my housing application.

About a month later I received a letter from them stating I was approved for a 2 bedroom apartment. It felt as though I had hit the lottery, because we were finally going to be living in a bigger place with less rent. I was receiving food stamps and a check because once my boyfriend started working I stayed at home with our son. When I went to look at our new home I found out that the rent was only 2 dollars. I couldn't have asked for nothing better if I tried. We immediately moved into our new home and soon after that my boyfriend found a job at a warehouse.

By him working on 3rd shift it seemed like we was straying apart. And one day I told him "That I had a dream he was cheating on me." And he said "I was just being paranoid", so I just pushed it out of my mind." Everything was going good for a while, until one day my sister and I was arguing and her husband said "My boyfriend was cheating on me with a woman at his job." I couldn't believe it after all we had been through I never thought he would ever cheat on me. But my brother in-law called the lady's house and asked for him and I put my ear to the phone. When I heard his voice I couldn't believe my ears; for a minute I was totally speechless and I said "You need to come home right now." When he arrived at the house I was standing outside mad as hell. I saw the window was rolled down and before he could put the car in gear I had reached in and slapped him. He jumped out of the car saying "I'm sorry" but it was too late for that. Because all I could think about is all the hell I went through trying to get him up here. And even though I didn't have a job, the next day I put him out. The next couple of weeks I went through pure hell and all I did was cry and listen to music. I had never felt this kind of pain before, and I didn't know how to handle it. I was young, hurt & alone and all I could think about was dying so I ended up trying to commit suicide. My sister came by and found me and called the suicide squad, they pumped my stomach and took all the sharp objects out of the house. And they told my sister "I needed to be watched closely," so she let me and my baby come stay with her for a while. By then my boyfriend had started coming by begging for forgiveness. He said "He didn't realize how much it would hurt to lose us," but I refused to take him back.

Time went by and I decided to get a job because I promised myself I would never depend on a man again. It was hard at first being alone but I was determined not to go backwards. But now I realize why my mother was so persistent on us knowing how to take care of ourselves. But one day I was sitting on my porch and saw this sexy guy riding back and forth on his motorcycle. My next door neighbor asked him "Did he see something he liked?" and he smiled. He then pulled over by the stairs and asked me "What was my name?" but by me still being hurt from my previous relationship I kind of shy'd away. But my neighbor knew I needed to go on with my life so she answered for me. He then said "Goodbye" and drove off, but the next day I was sitting outside by myself and he came over and started talking to me. We talked for a while and he asked enough questions to find out I had been scorned. But I guess that didn't matter because he asked "Could he come chill me the following day?" So the next day when he came by I introduced him to my son and we ended up talking throughout the night. Every day after that he started coming by and spending time with me and my son. It felt good to know that not only did he like me, but he was growing fond of my child also because I considered us a package deal. And besides he was handsome and had a job and those were two qualities a young girl looked for in a man. One night he came by and wanted us to take our friendship to another level, but I didn't know what to say because I still cared about my baby's dad. So I told him "Let's wait a little longer so I can be sure that this is what I wanted to do," and he agreed so we left it at that.

He came by the next day and asked me "To ride with him somewhere" and I asked "Where" and he said "You'll see when we get there," it turned out that he wanted me to meet his parents. And after that went alright, we planned a time for them to meet my son also. I knew he was getting more serious because he had started coming and checking on us every day.

One night after dinner we put my son to bed and went upstairs to watch television. While talking I told him "I hadn't thought about my baby's dad all day." But we both knew why and he reached over and kissed me.

Looking into my eyes he gently caressed my breast and asked "Did I think I was ready now." Before I could say anything my body responded for me, and we ended up making passionate love on the sofa. Early the next day he called and said "He enjoyed last night" and asked "Could he come by later," And I said "Yes." So later that day when he came by we were sitting in the living room and he was holding my son when my baby's father came by. I knew he was hurt because he didn't know I had met someone, and also that another man was holding his son. When I reached his son to him, he gave me this funny look as he took him outside on the porch.

The next morning my ex came by and started an argument about my friend holding his son. But I told him "That I had moved on with my life" and before I knew what happened he had slapped me and was throwing me around the living room. He said "I will never be with no one else." After he left I couldn't do nothing but cry, I started to call the police but I didn't want him to go to jail. When my friend came by I told him what had happened and he asked "Why didn't I call him," and at that moment my baby's dad came back. There was so much commotion going on but at the same time I was pleased to see that my friend was willing to fight for me.

My neighbors had called the police and I put a trespassing on my baby's father. That night my friend suggested "That it would probably be best if he started living us." Everything was going fine for a while, because the more I fell in love with my friend; the more my feelings faded away for my baby's father. But after a while my friend didn't want my baby's father to come by at all. But I didn't agree because even though we weren't together, I still felt he should be in his son's life.

Some months later my friend got a job at the same plant as my baby's dad and that's when things really started happening. By them working on different shifts when my friend was at work my ex would come by to see his son and eventually he started begging me to take him back. But the wounds were too deep for me to allow him back in my life, and besides I had just recently found out I was pregnant by my new friend. But because he was so jealous he kept me stressed out all the time and I ended up having a miscarriage. I was real sad for a while but 4 months later I found out I was pregnant again. But this time my boyfriend pampered me because he didn't want me to have another miscarriage. And on September20th 1991 I gave birth to a healthy baby boy. My baby's dad and my boyfriend had become friends by then and I was being treated like a queen, so I couldn't ask for a better life. Then one day my baby's father got threw out the house and he asked us "Could he stay with us for a while." We agreed that he could stay and sleep with his son, and pay toward rent and food until he can go back home." But I could feel the tension when we were all together because my friend knew my ex still loved me. My girlfriends thought it was hilarious that I had both my baby's fathers living with me at the same time. But the only reason I did this was because I brought him up here and I felt responsible, and besides he didn't have anywhere else to go. But after staying with us a month he went back home, but I know the real reason he left was because he couldn't handle seeing me sleeping with another man.

Shortly after he left he stopped all communication with me and his son. And about a year later I asked him for $20 to pay our sons school fees and he said "Let who you're sleeping with give it to you" so I ended up having to put him on child support. In the meantime my boyfriend had started drinking more heavier than usual, he said he had been under a lot of pressure lately but he promised he was going to quit. But instead things got worse and he would start fights for no reason at all. I was at the point where I was ready to leave him because I couldn't take it anymore. Then out of the blue he gave me an engagement ring and asked me to marry him, and because I still loved him I said "Yes." We were supposed to get married on July 24th because that's his birthday but two weeks before the wedding I decided I couldn't go through with it. I tried to sit down and explain to him why; but he didn't want to hear it. I still loved him but I knew in my heart he would never change at least not anytime soon, and sure enough things started getting worst. So one day while he was at work I packed my stuff and rented a U-Haul and moved to an apartment I had recently found in South Carolina.

It was hard living in a city with no family or friends but I had to try. I went and applied for DSS and food stamps, and I had an apartment on bus route so we had no problem with transportation. For amusement my boys and I would put clothes on and ride the city bus to the mall and back.

But one day I started running out of money and this guy that always sits outside my apartment called me over. He said "He noticed I've been having it hard and either I need a man to take care of me or make some money myself." And by me not being the type to sleep with men for money I decided to hustle. At the time I only had one of my sons with me because my oldest son's dad had asked me "To let our son stay in school in N.C while I get situated." And by me being young and not knowing any better I agreed. Everything was alright for a while, but one day I met this guy from N.Y and he offered me more money and I started selling for him. He would send me customers so I wouldn't have to leave home. It worked out fine because I made lots of money and was able to be at home with my baby.

One day I was offered 25,000 to make a trip to Florida and bring a package back to Spartanburg. And even though the money sounded good, I couldn't take a chance on getting a trafficking charge and being taken away from my son's. Things were going fine until one night I was putting away my stash, and this lady that I'd sold drugs too earlier had hid behind my door and cut my throat. I couldn't believe what was happening but I knew she was trying to kill me. She was planning on cutting my throat and stealing the drugs, but I started fighting back and when she let go I panicked and ran outside screaming. I had forgotten my baby was still in the house with this crazy woman. But by then the neighbors had called the police and when they arrived I was screaming telling them "To get my baby." After they kicked the door in and retrieved her they brought my baby down safely but I had to leave him with the neighbors so I could go to the hospital. Even though I had gotten my throat cut I found myself still thanking God that nothing had happened to my baby. I wasn't able to tell the police what really happened because I would have gotten in trouble, so I had to charge it to the game. But when I got home from the hospital and saw my baby, it dawned on me how I had put both our lives in danger. So I decided it was time for me to get out of this line of business.

I had a little money saved up so I found a job that was on bus route. My neighbor started keeping my son so I could work, and eventually I had enough money to purchase a cheap car. The transition was hard but I was determined not to go back to hustling, and besides I had promised my child I would never put him in danger again. As time went on my younger sister and her baby came to live with us. And we made an arrangement that I would watch the babies while she go to school and she would watch them when I go to work. It was hard at first though because I had just started working on a 3rd shift job. While I was at work I met this lady and she took a liking to me. She started calling me her daughter and would always cook dinner and bring me a plate to work. One day she told me she had a son in prison, but I didn't think anything of it until the day I saw them at Green Galaxy grocery store. I spoke and got her attention, so I could get a better look at her son. After she introduced him she went into the store. I chatted with him a minute and then gave him my number and told him to "Call me." I never knew this would be a major turning point in my life.

Later that night he called and asked "Could he come by," and I said "Yes" and immediately got ready for his visit. When he came by we sat in the living room for hours getting to know each other better. I learned he had just gotten out that day, but that didn't bother me because he was so sexy and on top of that I was lonely as hell. He asked me "To show him around" and when we got by the bedroom he motioned me to sit on the bed.

And then out of the blue he kissed me and started nibbling on my ears. I was about to burst inside but I tried to keep my composure because I had just met him. But he was very straight forward about the situation because he said "I know you think I only want to sleep with you, but I have no intentions of this just being a one night stand." And since he was so sexy and sincere I decided to take a chance; so I reached him a condom because I always practice safe sex. To say he had been locked up for 4 yrs. he was so gentle and his love making was the bomb. The next morning while he was asleep I peeked under the covers to get a look at his body. He had made me feel so good till I couldn't help but be curious. When he woke up I asked him "Did he need a ride home" and he said "Yes and could he come see me later." I said "Yes" and we kissed and said our goodbyes.

That evening my sister and I rode to North Carolina, and by the time we had gotten back home he had left about 20 messages. He was over whelming me by showing me so much attention. He came by and stayed the night and it seemed like every day after that he was staying the night.

Things were moving very fast but at the same time I was enjoying his company. In the meantime my sister had met a guy at a party, and all four of us started getting real close. Then one day my friend said "He may as well move in because he's already here all the time." And because I cared about him so much I agreed. Shortly after that my sister's newfound friend started staying with her also. Everything was going good but it was cramped with 4 adults and 3 children living in a 2 bedroom apartment. But a few months later my sister graduated and found an apartment and moved out.

After about 7 months had passed my friend proposed to me and we ended up getting married on September 17 at the Justice of the Peace. After we were married his mother and her boyfriend took us to Charlotte N.C for our honey moon. We had a great time but after we made it back home my husband started changing.

I began noticing a difference in my husband's attitude, and how his gentle nature had turned abusive. And one day $20 dollars came up missing from my purse, I called his mother and told her that "I believe he's stealing from me because no one was here but us." And later day she came by and gave me the money back. I thought that was rather strange unless she knew something that I didn't know. When my husband came home I noticed he had cut all his hair off. And when I brought it to his attention about the money he got real defensive. And by me being a country girl I didn't know how to recognize the signs of a drug user, so he was able to talk his way out of it. And later on I found out I was pregnant, but by this time my husband had started being abusive, I didn't understand why though because I was doing everything a wife should do. I knew something was wrong because my husband would come home and start fights for no reason at all. And about a few months later I started throwing up and before I knew it I was bleeding. I then went to the doctor and he said "I had a complete miscarriage." I cried and cried and later that day his mom stopped by and said "She needed to talk to me." She told me about how my husband had been to jail on several drug charges. And how he had gotten addicted on drugs since he was young. She went on to tell me about things he had done during his addiction. I couldn't believe what I was hearing it was as though I was caught in a nightmare. I was totally shocked because during the whole time we dated I never saw a sign that he had a problem, and besides he was the most considerate and gentlest man I'd ever known.

So how could he hide a dark secret like that from me all this time? By the time I found out about my husband's addiction we were about 1yr into our marriage, and despite how he had changed I was in love with him and leaving him wasn't an option. My life was crazy because here I am a young lady in love with an abusive man who has a drug addiction. I eventually became pregnant again but this time he wasn't fighting me he was running the streets every day. And because I was stressing so much it resulted in me losing our second child. He ultimately had started back using drugs and was out of control. It felt like I was living two separate lives, because when he wasn't using he was the best husband in the world but when he was using he took me through pure hell. But in my heart I knew I couldn't leave him if I wanted too, because I was all he had. He had become very controlling because he knew he would never find another woman like me again. So not only did his addiction make him abusive it made him sexually controlling also. I remember lying in bed crying all the time because I couldn't get any sleep. He would want to have sex constantly but I knew it was because of his addiction. And one day he came home high and out of the blue jumped on me for no reason and then went laid down and fell asleep. I couldn't take it anymore so I called the police and told them that he had been fighting me, and they came and awakened him while handcuffing him and took him to jail.

Later that night the police called and said he was about to be released. So me and my boys locked the doors and put the refrigerator behind it because we were scared and we knew he would come back. And then we went to the back room and sit on the bed. I told my oldest son "If his step dad comes here don't let him hurt me." And I told my youngest son "To hide beside the bed." Sure enough he came and kicked the door open and at that moment I dialed 911. He grabbed me by the throat and began choking me, and as I was blacking out I saw my oldest son grab a knife and start stabbing him. At that quick instant he let go of my neck and I caught a quick breath and grabbed a bat that was on the floor and started hitting him with it. And at that moment the police bust in and my husband ran into the closet. I was hysterical and was pointing in the direction where he was.

They pulled him out and because he was resisting, they began hitting him with their sticks and then they shackled him and took him to jail. I couldn't believe what had just happened, as it kept replaying over and over in my mind. I was so scared that my sons and I slept in the same room for two months. And every day I would call the Spartanburg Regional crisis center to talk to someone in trauma. And even though he was told not to contact me he did so anyway. He said "He was sorry and if I hadn't called the police he probably would've killed me." And by me having the kind of heart that I do over time I forgave him but I told him I couldn't be with him anymore. But regardless of what he had done I knew he loved me and I loved him too but life goes on.

Eventually I went to the solicitor's office and told them I didn't want to press charges, "Because even though he tried to hurt me I didn't want to see him locked up for life." I didn't know if it would help him get his life together, but I felt like he deserved to have a second chance. Everyone thought I was crazy for dropping the charges, but something in my heart wouldn't let me do it. After that my sons and I went on with our lives, and over a period of time we were able to forget what happened that night.

Eventually my husband was released from jail and called me from his mother's house "To thank me for dropping the charges." But fortunately I wasn't home and the answering machine caught the message, because I still didn't want any dealings with him whatsoever.

It had now turned summer and I went to Dollar General to buy my son's some water guns, and while I was there this guy started talking to me.

And after leaving the checkout line he asked "For my number" and I smiled and hesitantly gave it to him. The next day he called and we went out to dinner, and I was shocked at how much I enjoyed myself. After that 3 days passed and I hadn't seen or heard from him, so I assumed he wasn't interested. But a few days later I received a phone call and it was him, he had gone to jail right after our visit. He evidently was dealing with someone and they had gotten in a fight and she had him locked up. After we hung up the phone I went to the county jail and bailed him out, I had no reason for doing it I just felt compelled to help him. We then started seeing each other more and more and then one day I made the mistake of sleeping with him.

And afterwards I found out he was an acquaintance of my husband. That really made me feel bad because I never wanted to hurt my husband by dealing with a man that he knew. And after my husband found out who he was they stayed into arguments all the time.

My friend and I were together about a year before I found out who he really was. I had been hearing different things about him, but I didn't want to believe it. So I found out the hard way that he didn't like to work and that he was an alcoholic. And because he wasn't helping me pay the bills I eventually joined a card club. My friend had become very controlling and every time he would drink he'd start a fight. I use to go to work with black eyes because I wouldn't agree on something he said. Our relationship was getting worse by the day, I would go gamble just so I wouldn't have to be at home dealing with him. And one night he came home drunk and told me "If I wasn't happy just let him know and he'll leave," and when I said "I wasn't happy" he grabbed a knife and cut me across my arm. And when my husband found out what he had done he "Dared him to meet him some place." Because even though he had been abusive he wasn't going to stand by and let another man hurt me. I was sick of this relationship and just wanted to get out, but it wasn't that easy because he was dependent on me, and wasn't about to just let me go. So for a while I dwelled from day to day in this living nightmare.

One day while we were at his sister's house a girl came by, and I found out he had been sleeping with her. She thought I was going to fight her but I was actually happy. I left him there and immediately went home and started packing his stuff. Even though I was a little hurt I was happy that God was finally moving him out of my life. I then vowed I would stop dealing with men for a while, and take some time out for myself. And that's when I realized my gambling had gotten out of control, because I was spending $4 to 5 hundred dollars a week playing cards and pulling ball tickets. I had stopped paying my bills and it seemed like we were getting an eviction notice every other month. And eventually I started going straight to card games right after work. My oldest son had to make sure his younger brother ate and got out to school, because I would normally come in late and be to sleepy to do anything. And on top of that I was stopped one day for speeding and found out my license was under suspension. I was given a ticket for $647 for driving under suspension and $74 for speeding. But I still had to get to work so I kept driving and a few days later I got stopped again. This time not only did I receive a ticket but they towed my car. And by me having a gambling addiction I couldn't pay my tickets so I got my oldest son to drive me to my card games on his permit. And about a month later my landlord started tripping and put us out. So we ended up putting our furniture in storage and staying in a hotel.

I cried every time I thought about my husband and how he would've never let us live like this. I realized I had let things get too far out of hand, but I didn't know what to do. Because despite my husband's addiction he always made sure we were taken care of. And right now I felt so alone and would've given anything for him to be here, but unfortunately he wasn't and I was on my own. It tore me up inside to see what I was putting my children through, so I began looking for a cheap place. Because I knew they would rather be anywhere than staying in a hotel room. God finally blessed me to find a reasonable place, and I talked to the owner and told her my situation and she rented it to me.

Soon after we moved in I had to go to court for my tickets and I was given 2 days to pay all the money or they were going to lock me up. It felt like my world was coming to an end, because

I didn't have anyone to look after my children if I got locked up. The next day I was leaving work early and gave my number to a co-worker that I associated with, and told him my situation. And I told him that if I didn't come back to work I wanted him to check on my children for me. But after work he called me and told me to meet him at his bank. Even though I didn't know why me and my boys rushed over there. When we arrived he told me "To come to his car so he could talk to me for a minute." He had an envelope in his hand with the money I needed to pay my fine and then some. I just stood there crying as he was telling me "There was no strings attached and that he couldn't see me go to jail because my kids needed me." He said "I could just pay him back little by little when I could." I couldn't believe that someone would ever do something like this for me.

Everything was going fine for a while, even my husband's mother started coming by and asking me "Would I go to a visit with her." And I would tell her "Yes" but when the time came I'd change my mind. He had been locked up about 4 yrs. and I really wanted to see him, but I couldn't forget all the pain he had put me through during our marriage. But it's funny how I never divorced him, even though we had been separated for years. But I knew the reason why; it was because deep in my heart I still loved him. But I couldn't see us in a relationship again, because I didn't believe he would ever change. But the reason I believe none of my other relationships worked was because no one could take his place in my heart.

During this time I was trying to stop gambling, because I wanted to be a better mother for my sons. And one day my sister in-law called and asked me "To go to church with her", and even though I was planning to go to the club that night I went on and accepted. That night it seemed like the preacher was just talking to me and I gave my life to Christ. It seemed like everything started changing after that and I began seeing things in a totally different way. I realized after all this time all I had to do was call on Jesus and he would make everything alright. My mother in-law as usual came by and asked me "About visiting my husband" and I said "yes" but this time I had the intentions of actually going. The next morning when she arrived she was shocked to see that I was up and ready. I hadn't seen or talked to him since he went to prison, so I knew this would be an interesting visit.

When we arrived inside the prison he was standing in a line with several other men. When he saw me come through the door he looked as though he'd seen a ghost. And he smiled and embraced me as if he was seeing was I real. That moment touched my heart when I noticed the tears in his eyes. The visit went better than I expected, it was as if I had been around the whole time. And during the ride home I realized my feelings for him was still there. A couple of months later he was released from prison and started living with his mom. We talked on the phone every day and one night he asked "Could he come chill with me." I was kind of hesitant but I told him "Yes." As we was sitting in my living room he began telling me that he hadn't been with anyone since he came home, because he still cared about me. And he asked "Could he stay the night because he just wanted to hold me again." That night we ended up making passionate love, it felt like it did when we first fell in love. He eventually started asking me "What was we going to do about us," but I was confused at what was happening, so I told him I think right now it's best if he stayed at his moms.

A few days later I called him and he sounded nervous, and I asked him "Did he have company." And hesitantly he said "Sort of" so I said "Ok" and hung up the phone. I didn't understand what had come over me, because it felt as though he was cheating on me or something. If I had a car that day I would of went over there and did something crazy, because after all the hell he had put me through he wasn't going to disrespect me like that. He was with his mother when she came to take me to the doctor the next day, and the more I thought about him talking to another woman the madder I got. And before I knew it I had reached across the seat and slapped him, not caring about what may happen, because by law he was still legally my husband. After that I didn't talk to him for a while, because I wanted him to feel the same way he had made me feel. We eventually got back together, but we had some serious trust issues to work out.

During this time I had begun falling behind again on my rent, and my husband found us an apartment by his mother. Things were fine for a while until he went back to his old ways, and started running the streets.

Me and a couple from church ran behind him and prayed for him every day.

My pastor even went picked him up a few times and brought him home. He would always stop for a minute and then start right back. Eventually he got back in trouble with the law and was sent back to jail. About a month later I got him out and I decided to find a cheaper place that I could afford by myself. We ran across this cheap little brick house in Whitney, it had holes in the walls and mildew in every bedroom, but we turned it into our new home. Everything was fine for a while until my husband started working for one our neighbors. He was a contractor and he would take my husband with him to do yard work. But because of my husband's addiction, when he got paid he wouldn't come home. I was too ashamed to tell anyone so I just tried to maintain the best I could. And over time it only got worse, because one day he left and didn't come back for about a month. And when he did come home he would always steal something and end up leaving again. And every time he did this he would come and beg me not to leave him, and because I felt sorry for him I wouldn't.

By now my two sons was holding resentment toward him, because they felt like he was only dragging me down. But to me it felt as though some kind of force was keeping me from walking away. But after a while I had a change of heart, and stopped looking for him when he pulled his disappearing acts. And one day his mother called and said "He was back in jail," but at this point it was somewhat a relief because I had been asking "God to keep him covered." And anyway I had made myself a promise "That the next time he left he'd have to prove to me he wanted to be in this marriage." So I decided to start doing things with the church in hope I could see a change in my life. I started going to prayer services, revivals and any other events that could help me in what I was going through. My daily prayer consisted of my husband getting his deliverance, so that we could make our marriage work. Well months went by and my husband finally got out of jail, and that night he came to the house and after talking awhile we ended up making love. It felt good waking up in his arms again but I still didn't know how I allowed this to happen. And for a while he did everything in his power to show me how much he loved me. And because he was such a humble and good hearted person, I eventually found myself falling back in love with him.

But it wasn't too long after he gained my heart back that he began using drugs again. I couldn't believe it; he had just done 4 yrs. and on top of that God had given him his family back. But now his addiction was ten times worse and he went on with his life as if I didn't exist. I thank God that I was saved because it helped me look at things in an entirely different way.

And I realized that it wasn't him it was the demonic spirits that was holding him bound. We had been going to church at Bountiful Blessing and with the help of my pastor and church family; I was able to make it through this ordeal. We kept him in daily prayer and every now and then we would find him, and clean him up and get him back in church. This had become a cycle but it was important to keep nurturing the word into his spirit man. It seemed as though this went on forever but one day my prayers were answered, and after a fifteen year crack addiction my husband had finally started receiving his deliverance. I couldn't believe it, but I was actually seeing him walking in his deliverance for the first time during our marriage.

But he was worried about a charge he had obtain while he was on the streets, and I reassured him that if he stayed faithful God would work it out.

And besides God had already given him his family back and most of all he had Gods favor on his life. He really tried to stay in good standing with God, but sometimes he'd get weak and let the enemy pull him away.

At this point the enemy was using my husband and anyone else he could to detour me. Because one day my next door neighbor came by and asked "Did I want to come to a card game and I told her "No" I've been set free from gambling." It was unbelievable because it felt like I'd never gambled before in my life. But I knew God had removed that desire, because I hadn't gambled since March of 2005, and it was now August 2007. And that's why I know when God sets you free you're free indeed.

Around this time my husband had another relapse, but this time when he fell he had Gods word to stand on. So I stepped aside and watched God work in his life. And besides on August 9th my 1st grand baby was born and my son and his girlfriend were having problems, so I had to deal with that also. But I knew at this point what I had to do and that was to intercede for my family. And by me being the prayer warrior in the family I had to constantly stay on my knees. So I began seeking spiritual guidance from my pastor, and reading spiritual books including the bible. I still wanted to leave my husband, but every time I thought about doing it God would touch my heart. So I just made it up in my mind that I wouldn't worry about anything he did, because I knew in my heart God was telling me to just stay prayed up and be still.

My husband later became an armor barrier at church, because he wanted to stay close under the anointing of our pastor. And it showed me the kind of man he could be if he walked in Gods footsteps. But I had to come to realization that he would keep falling until he totally surrenders to God, and as long as he's a weak vessel I'll have to continue standing in prayer for the family. I'm finally seeing my blessings manifest, because even though I have bad credit I've been blessed with a 2000 expedition and I'm still believing God for a home. And my youngest son has passed to the 11th grade, and I'm praying that God keep his covering over each of our lives. At this point I'm not only praying for my husband, but I'm praying that my brother and my oldest son turn their lives over to Christ also. And even though my family is going through a terrible storm right now, I know that at the end of every storm there's a rainbow.

I'm still at Siemens 11yrs later and I consider that a blessing, because no one knows the trials I've endured since I've been working there. And even though a lot of people are celebrating that I've changed, I still have my haters. But that's because they can't accept the fact that I don't do the things I use too. I even see God blessing my finances, by giving me plenty opportunities for overtime. That's why I'm trying my best to live the right way because I want everything he has for me. And even though my husband is still running the streets, I'm going to continue standing still because I know one day God will reveal the purpose he has for my life. But I really need things to change in my marriage because I can't keep living this way.

And if my husband doesn't get his self together and start helping me, I'm going to eventually end up by myself.

Well it's 2008 and my husband and I have separated, and now I'm focusing on letting God work on me. So I've decided to get involved in different ministries, because where God is trying to take me I'm going to need all the spiritual knowledge I can get. I know this will be a long and hard road but I can do all things through Christ that strengthen me. But tomorrow will be a new day for me, because I'll be entering an isolation period with only God. It's amazing how you have to be fed up with something before you can give it to God. And even though my flesh still desires attention, I had come to the realization that I must live as a Christian woman or I would be bound for hell. So I began reading the bible trying to get an understanding of what my father wants me to do. God has spared my life so many times so I know he has a purpose for me. That's why I asked him "To remove my sexual desires so I could focus strictly on him," and he did "Praise God" and from that moment on my life was never the same.

Over time I started praying for God "To send a good God filled man into my life" and he sent my husband back. I didn't understand why but I didn't question it either, because I know God has a reason for everything he do. It's amazing how God works; he knew I still cared about my husband and he gives you what the heart desire. My church family and I kept him in prayer, but eventually he got in trouble again and went back to jail. But I always told him "Warning comes before destruction," and God had to isolate him to get his full attention. But this time my husband said "Something was different," and he started reading the bible and accepting what God wanted to do in his life. But while he was in jail I kept praying for him, because one thing I know is that a believing wife can intercede for an unbelieving husband. And at the same time that God was working on him he was also working on me, and he was showing me that everything that I was going through during my marriage was getting me ready for what he wanted me to do. When my husband got out he went back to being an armor barrier and I became an usher and an intercessor. We were on fire for the Lord, and he was really using us in his kingdom. And now we understood what the phrase meant "Greater is he that's in us than he that's in the world." It just took us a while to realize that what we want is not always what God wants.

We later decided it would be a good idea to relocate from the middle of Spartanburg. So we found a nice duplex in Boiling Springs where my family and I resided for a while. And even though it was a nice neighborhood our situations didn't change very much. And regardless of how hard my son and brother saw we were having it, they still weren't ready to give their lives to Christ. And even though I knew it was wrong I found myself questioning Gods word, because I didn't understand why I had to deal with so many problems? But I knew there had to be a reason for everything I'm going through I just haven't figured it out yet. But at the same time I can see the favor God has on my life, and how he's constantly blessing me. Because at one point I had to catch rides to work, but now I have two vehicles in my yard. And he's taking people out of my life and replacing them with people that can help me in this walk. That's why I'm going to keep on praying and pressing my way until my life is complete.

Time has passed and my youngest son is about to go to the 12th grade, I still treat him like a baby even though he's almost a man. And not only am I interceding for my family, but I'm praying and fasting also. Because some yokes can only be broken through fasting and prayer, and this is the year of new beginnings and that means God is going to put some things behind us.

We were finally blessed with a house in September and even though it was expensive it was still a gift from God. And the time had come for my husband to go to court for an old charge, and he was really scared because he was facing 15yrs. but I knew God would meet him at his point of need.

When he went to court me and some of our church family went to support him, and we witnessed a miracle happen before our very eyes. He ended up getting a 15yr sentence suspended to 3yrs probation, and not having to serve one day of jail time. We all went back to the church to pray and thank God for the miracle we had just witnessed. As I laid on the floor I began to cry and immediately went into a state of concentration, because after witnessing a miracle like that I couldn't help but give God the highest praise.

It was now time for us to move into our new home. And my husband's mother asked "Could she come live with us because she no longer wanted to live by herself." So I said "Yes" because not only was she my husband's mother, but I looked at her as a mother figure also. And my youngest son was going to the 12th grade so I bought him an 86 Crown Victoria as a gift, and I let my oldest son fiancé come stay with us until he got out of jail. I can't make decisions for my sons I can only raise them the best that I can.

Because it's hard enough for a woman to raise a boy less known teach him how to be a man. As for my husband I bought him a boat and a pool table so he could have something to keep him occupied but that wasn't enough, because he eventually started easing back toward the streets. Our marriage was really suffering and everyone in the family was walking around with hostility in their hearts, because whenever something came up missing he'd always claim he didn't see it. Time went by and our family situation had gotten worse, because no one ever knew when my husband would come home high. I often wondered what was keeping me from leaving him but I couldn't put my finger on it.

But I did know that I was getting tired of this cycle, and eventually I would have to make a decision.

So in the meantime everyone just hid their belongings and went on like normal, until one day something happened that I didn't expect. I was ironing a dress for church and my mother-in-law was in her room looking at television, and my youngest son was outside working on the radio in his car when my husband arrived. He came in the house and asked me for "The title to his boat" and by me knowing he wanted to sell it I told him "No". I should have noticed something was about to happen because he started pacing back and forth around the room. He then walked over by me and started demanding his title and once again I refused and he grabbed my head and slammed it against the bed post. He then pushed my head against the wall and started choking me. As we was fighting his mother ran in the room and tried to stop him and he pushed her out of the way. So she ran back to her room and called 911. He then ran out of our bedroom into her room and pushed her down on the bed and hung up the phone. When he re-entered our bedroom I immediately struck him with the iron and we began fighting again. But he knew that the law would be coming soon so he emptied my purse and grabbed my truck keys. He then ran outside and I ran behind him screaming for him "To give me my keys." But he ignored me and jumped into the truck, and as he was starting it up I grabbed the driver door. He then put it in reverse and hit the gas and slung me to the ground and as I was rolling on the concrete my son saw what had happened and immediately jumped in his car in pursuit of my husband.

By this time the police had arrived, and was checking me out because I was bleeding very badly. They were also in pursuit, because my son was still chasing my husband on the other side of town. When the rest of my family heard about what had happened they were furious. They said "His mother should leave," because they didn't want any part of his family around. So she moved in with one of her daughters to keep down confusion.

Even though everyone was upset his mother actually saved my life. I was scared to death because out of all the times I've been abused something about this time was different. I actually saw my life pass before my eyes and I knew that if I didn't make a decision now I would end up dying from physical abuse.

So I started looking for a place where my husband wouldn't know where I was. When I found a convenient spot that was hid off the road I started moving my furniture during the night so it would look like I was still there. Then I eventually relocated and no one but my immediate family knew where I was. It was hard going day to day trying to keep everyone from knowing where I lived, but after what had happened I didn't know who I could trust. It seemed like forever before I could feel comfortable staying at home alone. I parked my vehicles in the back of the house and I couldn't have anyone over to talk too, so it felt like I was in hiding. But I realized God was trying to isolate me for some reason, so I didn't worry about anything that went on around me. For about five months my schedule was going to work and on Sunday going to church and spending time with my puppy. I'm really grateful that God had allowed me to have something in my life that could give me some kind of comfort. And since my sons were busy with their own lives, my life only consisted of God and my puppy.

But during the time I was away from my husband I heard through the grapevine that he had started living with another woman. For some strange reason I felt hurt, because I couldn't believe after all these years it was that easy to be with another woman and forget about me. But even though I was hurt it still wasn't enough to make me want him back. I decided to just let go and let God have his way. And one night I was sitting at home reading my bible and started crying, and asked God "Why was I going through all this?" And all of a sudden it felt as though I had slipped into a deep sleep. I then heard a voice as though someone was talking to me in a conversation. So I started writing down what I was hearing because I had never experienced this before and I didn't want to forget anything. The next day I started writing my feelings on paper and they began to form into poems. My 1st poem was titled "A Born Conqueror" and it stated "That this would be the turning point in my life." I shared it with my family members and they said it was amazing, and my sister in law said "That I should talk to someone about my poems." So after that I began writing all the time, it felt as though my pain was pouring out like a river. Before I knew it I had written about fifty poems and each one was just as powerful as the next.

People had started telling me" How touching my poems were" and even my pastor said "This was truly my calling." And before I knew it I had written over three hundred poems within five months. I then seeked a publishing company to look at my work, and they loved it. It was amazing because along with writing all these poems, I had gotten a book published and a website started in less than a year.

Only God could make something that wonderful happen so quick. So I allowed him use me but made sure he was given the glory. I also made business cards to give out to everyone so they could see the gift that was placed in me. Everything was moving so fast and I was constantly being blessed; for a minute I even forgot about all the hurt and pain I've endured.

I just kept my faith and believed that God would work everything out for me. One day I met a lady at an event and we immediately became friends. She asked me "To come to her house for a cook out," at first I hesitated but then decided to go and get out of the house for a while. I never knew what made me accept her invitation because at the time I'd gone nine months without being with a man, or even going anywhere I would end up meeting one. I had given up on ever finding love again, but at the same time I was thankful I had found it in God. When I arrived at the cookout I saw a lot of people and I almost didn't want to get out of the car. But when I decided to go in a guy walked up to me and I told him who I was looking for, and he said "She was inside the house." So when I got inside she smiled because she was glad to see me and told me "To have a seat and get something to eat." While she was preparing the food two guys came in the house and she introduced them to me as her sons. It was awkward because one of them was the guy that walked up to me when I first pulled up.

Well later on after I had eaten and left, I was back at home getting prepared for church the next day when my phone rung. When I answered it I wasn't surprised that a man's voice was on the other line, because I had given out cards about my books and I assumed it was someone inquiring about my work. But it was totally the opposite the voice on the phone was one of the guys from the cookout. He said "I met him" but I wasn't talking to any guys so I couldn't place him. Then he said he was my friends' oldest son and he had gotten my number off the card I had given her. He asked "Could he take me out to dinner and get to know me a little better, but by me not wanting to deal with any men's right now I began making excuses. I told him "I was flattered that he was attracted to me but I didn't really want to date anyone right now." But he was very persistent and didn't seem like he was trying to give up that easy, because when I told him that I was going to church he asked "What about after service then?" And then I told him that I was going to a second service and he then said "Well could I call him after that service" and I said "I guess."

The next day after second service as I was leaving church my phone rung and it was him calling to see if I would meet him for dinner. I was hoping he had forgotten but I see he hadn't, because he called me instead of waiting on me to call him. So I accepted and we decided to go to a movie because I wanted to be around other people. We didn't get to see very much of the movie, because our conversation had gotten interesting and we found out we had a lot in common. Our date went very well and he carried himself like a perfect gentleman. I couldn't believe he didn't say anything wrong the whole night, so I decided to see him again. It seemed like every day before I got off work, he had already planned something for us to do. It really made me feel good for someone to show me so much attention. And when I asked him "To go to church with me" he agreed and that meant a lot to me, because anyone I allowed in my life at this point would have to love God as much as I do. About two months passed and everything was going great, but my friend began inquiring about us taking our friendship to another level. Even though I cared a lot about him I still wasn't ready to sleep with anyone quite yet.

The few weeks later we went to a Steelers game, and after returning home he asked "Could he stay the night" and I said "Yes." That night we made passionate love and he then said "He wanted us to become an item." I was happy but at the same time confused at what I was doing. Because I was still legally married and trying to write books showing the goodness of God. But my flesh got the best of me and I chose to enter into a relationship. Everything was wonderful at first, but then our lives took a turn for the worst. The police bust into my house looking for one of my sons, and a blunt was on the weight bench down stairs. And since it was my house they said "They had to charge me with it." And a couple days later they came back and took both my sons to jail and my landlord told me "I had to move." I wasn't prepared for any of this so my friend and I had to go stay in a hotel where we had to pay a weekly rate. We ended up staying there about 8 months, before finding a cheap trailer to move in.

A year after the incident they dropped the charges because they knew they wouldn't stick. But since my youngest son had received 18 months, there was no way I could ever leave my baby boy behind, so I just dealt with whatever I had to in order to make it. It was hard at first because my son had never been away from me, and he would cry every time I went to visit him. But we made it through that period with the help of the good Lord.

Around this time my friend had started hanging out at liquor houses and in trap houses. I told him "That I can't be seen in those types of places, because doing that time I was promoting my books and doing poetry readings at different church functions. And besides "I didn't drink or smoke, so why would I want to be seen in those kinds of places anyway?"

And later I found out he was cheating with a girl at one of the liquor houses.

He started coming in late or sometimes not at all, and I was getting real tired of it. I latter found out he had started hustling again and when I confronted him "He denied it." He tried to get me to believe that everyone was jealous of him and that's why they were lying. But one day someone came to our house and I saw him reach them something, and after they left I went off on him. He told me that "He loved me but he needed to make him some extra money and why can't I accept him for who he is?" and I told him "I just can't and that I didn't think it would work out between us because we're going two different directions."

After that night things only got worse and my friend then started hustling out in the open. He no longer cared if I could deal with it or not, so I decided that it was time for me to leave. I didn't want to get caught up in a drug bust of any kind, especially not one dealing with large quantities of hard drugs. He thought I was bluffing, until the day he came home and saw it was empty. I had taken everything and put it in storage except his belongings. By this time my son had come home from prison and he had met a girl in the trailer park, so he started staying with her and I went stayed with my oldest son's baby's mother. My days consisted of going to work, church and taking my son where he needed to go. As time went on the wounds began to heal and I soon realized I wasn't hurting anymore.

And just as I was getting my life back together my oldest son went to prison. I couldn't believe this was happening all over again, because I rejoiced one coming home for the other to be taken away. I often wondered "Why was this happening to me?" "What is it I've done so terrible that I deserve to get punished like this?" he was gone for a few months then they brought him back to a facility in Spartanburg. I was so happy because I had access to visit him every weekend and besides he was at home. While he was there I soon found out his step father was there also. Because he called me one day and told me "That his step father wanted to speak to me", I was hesitant but said "Ok." When I heard his voice it felt like something went through my stomach. It was such a loving and familiar voice, and my heart immediately begin melting. He asked me "Could I come see him sometimes at the prison?" and I said "I'll see." That weekend my son's girlfriend went to visit him, and I visited my husband because that way we all could be in the visitation room at the same time. It was very awkward seeing him after all this time, especially knowing how it ended. He was smiling so hard when he saw me you'd think he won a million dollars. That day we didn't talk about anything dealing with the past, but we felt it would eventually have to be addressed. But for right now we just enjoyed the moment, and caught up on what's been going on in our lives. Between him and my son it seemed like I was visiting the prison every weekend.

Until one day my son was caught with some head phones and sent to another facility, where he was put on restrictions and stripped of his visitations for a year. But for some odd reason I still continued to visit my husband, because I knew there had to be a reason for us reconnecting after all this time. Every visit he would tell me "How blessed he was that I was there," and "How sorry he was for the things he had done to me." Just sitting there listening to him, made me realize how much I had missed him, but I couldn't let him know that. It's amazing after all this time his love for me has never changed. I continued visiting him every weekend, especially since I needed someone to talk to also. And I knew he would listen to anything I had to say, just as long as I was there. The weeks turned into months and now a year has passed and I'm still going to his visits.

3yrs. has passed since my first book was published, and I've just starting back writing. I guess all my questions have been answered and I've finally realized my purpose in life. Every visit my husband inquires about my books and that alone keeps me motivated. That's one of the qualities I've always adored about him, he's always interested in everything I do.

We've been talking about getting back together for a while now, and every day it's looking more and more promising. The more we talk the more I see how God is moving in his life. And I realize that everything that's happened was just Gods way of birthing forth the books he had placed in me. I believe "Poetry for the soul" volume 1, 2 and 3 will become best sellers because they are based on the unconditional love of two of Gods children. And now I can close this chapter of my life, because my search for love is over; I've finally found love in GOD and in MAN!

Written By Janice Stampley Means

About The Author

*J*anice Stampley Means was born in Natchez, Mississippi and currently resides in Boiling Springs, S.C. She is an active member of Bountiful Blessing Pentecostal Church under pastorship of Thomas J. Lee.

Janice is an encouraging speaker and author of four books titled "Poetry"

For The Soul volume 1, 2 and 3 and her autobiography titled "A Search for Love"

She's very inspiring to others when she speaks at church functions and many other events. Janice and her husband, Frederick, and her two sons, James and Mark live in Boiling Springs, S. C.

To contact Janice for speaking engagements

Iuniverse.com

(864)279-7843

Printed in the United States
By Bookmasters